DEBT SUCKS!

*Everyone's Guide To Winning With Money
So They Can Live Their Dreams*

JA'NET ADAMS

Dedication

The first thank you always goes to God because without Him none of this is possible! None of the books, none of the speaking engagements, and none of the television appearances. His gift truly makes room! Thank you to my family for always supporting me. My husband Jon as well as my children Jonathan (J.R.) and Jocelyn who keep me going as my daily inspiration. To my mother who taught me always to do my best no matter the circumstances and to hold my head high in the face of adversity I thank you

Thank you to my mother in law and father in law Patsy and Ronald Adams for always supporting the Debt Sucks movement and for helping out in any way you could! To my brothers Barry, Chris, and James who have been my protectors all my life, thank you for always coming to my rescue! To the multitude of friends and supporters this book and the Debt Sucks Movement would not be possible without your continued support!

Table of Contents

Chapter One

The Day Everything Changed

I couldn't believe what I was hearing. I was being laid off after eight years at this company. I had won numerous awards and earned bonuses year after year, but none of that mattered now because my services no longer needed. I felt defeated, like I had lost the biggest game of my life. Little did I know that my biggest challenge was waiting to be discovered. From the day I graduated college, I had a steady paycheck. Every two weeks I could count on a direct deposit to my bank account. This company that just laid me off also had great health insurance, gave me a company car to drive, and provided gas for the car as long as I was employed.

Now the car, gas, health insurance, and money were gone. Have you heard the saying "here today, gone tomorrow" Well, I experienced "here today, gone today" because I was laid off at 8:30AM and everything was gone by 5PM! The next day I found myself with no car, no health insurance, and no idea where my next paycheck was going to come from. I spent most of the day feeling sorry for myself because like so many other people, I had let my job define who I was. Now that I didn't have it anymore, I felt that I had lost my identity.

For eight years I had spent eight plus hours a day working and now with nothing to do, I started to open up bill statements. I opened up the energy bill, the water bill, the cell phone bill, the natural gas bill, the cable bill, and the mortgage. For the first time I was actually taking notice of how much our everyday necessities were costing to maintain. After seeing those numbers, I found the car and student loan payment envelopes and that is when worry started to set in.

Debt Sucks A-ha's

1. Your job is not your identity.

2. Don't go through life not knowing how much it costs to live each month.

3. Open up your bill statements every month.

Chapter Two

How Did We Get Here?

I met Jon in my freshman year in high school, but it would take until our senior year in high school for us to be a couple. We were both athletes and the sports that we were participating in since elementary school were supposed to be our one way ticket to a free college education. I went to college and played tennis for four years and he played basketball. Within a couple of years of graduating from college we were married, but when we walked down the aisle I did not know that he had a student loan debt of $25,000 for one year of college. He and I both thought he went to this college on a full-ride basketball scholarship, but that was not the case. The college's basketball coach had actually convinced his parents that he should go to this university and pay for his tuition out of pocket.

The only problem with that idea is that Jon's family didn't have $25K sitting in the bank, so they had to borrow the money through student loans—student loans that would have to be paid back in full! We were already married when I found this out and truth be told, Jon didn't know the amount of debt he had in student loans because up until the day we said "I do," the student loan bill was being mailed to his parent's house. The moment he told me he was thousands of dollars in debt, my heart sank. See, I had gone to college on a full scholarship, which means that everything that had to do with college was paid for in full. My housing was free, my food was free, my tuition was free, and my books were free. I didn't have to pay a dime to attend college. I graduated from college with no debt and even had a few thousand dollars in a savings account at the bank. So, up until the moment he told me the amount he owed in student loans, I thought we were newlyweds with the whole world in front of us, but in reality we were at the bottom of a hill, with a fight in front of us.

I thought that sinking feeling would never go away, but a stronger feeling soon took over and that was the feeling of impatience. Even though I had just walked down the aisle a couple of months before, I felt that it was time to move out of our apartment and into a house, not just any house—I wanted my dream home. I wanted this home to be bigger than our parent's homes so it could show that we had made it. At that time we had no business buying a home. We had only been married and living together in our first apartment for two months. We were not ready to take such a big step, but when you are a part of the "microwave generation," being ready doesn't matter. What is the microwave generation? It is exactly what it sounds like. You put a frozen meal in the microwave and two minutes later dinner is served—that is how I was living my life. This mentality had me thinking that our two-bedroom, two-bathroom apartment was too small. It had me thinking that if I can afford this apartment, a few hundred dollars more each month wasn't much if it meant owning my own home.

I immediately went and bought a book full of blueprints for homes. I spent hours each day searching through the 500-page book for the perfect home. When I finally found my dream home, I ordered the blueprints immediately and started searching for a contractor. As I was doing all of this, Jon was asking me, "Why the rush?" I would tell him, "I am not rushing. We are married and we need a house." I ignored his comments about the student loan because in my head it was HIS student loan, and HIS money needed to pay for it. His debt had nothing to do with this house being built. Eventually, I found a contractor and the land for the house. Within a year of getting married, we were in our new home. Everything was going great for an entire year and then one day Jon went outside to start his car. After a few failed attempts, it was clear to both of us that his car, a 2001 Mazda Millennia, needed to be repaired, so we took it to the mechanic and got it fixed.

After the car was fixed, I remember opening his car loan the next month and seeing how much was owed. He only owed about $3000 and his payments were low, but most of the payment was going to interest. I felt he was getting ripped off by the bank because the interest rate was so high. We could have easily solved that problem by going to the bank and refinancing to a lower interest rate, but instead I convinced Jon to go to the Chrysler dealership and trade in his almost paid off car for a $25,000 brand new, all white Chrysler 300. As we rode off the car lot, I looked Jon lovingly in the eyes and made sure he knew that the car was HIS car and that HIS paycheck would pay for it. Two years into our marriage, I still had not grasped the concept of what the preacher said on our wedding day: "Now you are one," which means HIS debt was OUR debt.

At this point it would seem logical that we would realize that we were now $50,000 in debt, not including our house, but no, we didn't even blink an eye at it. As long as the money was coming in, and all the bills were being paid, we were good. We continued to go on vacations every year, out to dinner three times a week, bought clothes, shoes, and every new electronic device that came out. Each time we went on vacation, we were not thinking that the money could have been used to pay down our debt. All we were thinking was that we needed vacations and needed to relax.

I think life decided that I was not paying enough attention, so it slapped me in the face with the loss of my job. When you go to no income, or in our case a one-income household, you start to look back on all the money you wasted and on all the clothes you bought and barely wore. You start to count all the times you went out to eat when you could have cooked. You realize that you could have driven that old car a little while longer. All of these thoughts ran through my head, but they quickly stopped when I saw the numbers on the car and student loans: $25,000 and $25,000 = $50,000 of debt; $50,000 that we owed other people. To complicate the situation even more, we had a one-year-old child staring us in the face with a look that basically said, "What are you going to do now?"

That is when I woke up. I realized that up until that moment, I thought I was the smartest person in the world when it came to money, but in reality, I was clueless. I thought I was winning by building the house because I was saving money on the construction, but the smart move was not to buy a house in the first place. I thought I was hurting the bank by trading in Jon's old car with the high interest rate for a new car, but the intelligent decision would have been to fix the car, drive it a few years more until we were able to buy a used car for cash. Bad financial decision after bad financial decision had put us in a deep hole, and it was going to take a lot to dig ourselves out and build a solid financial foundation going forward. It took me two-and-a half years to pay the $50,000 of debt off, and you can pay your debt off too but you have to be ready to completely rethink how you behave with money. Are you ready? Let's GO!

Debt Sucks A-ha's

1. Fixing a used car will always be cheaper than buying a new car.

2. When two people are married, "his debt" and "her debt" become "OUR DEBT."

3. Don't let a layoff force you to get control of your finances. Be proactive.

Chapter Three

Time to Dream Again

When we were kids, nothing was impossible. We dreamed we could be astronauts, kings and queens of our own country, superheroes, etc. The sky was the limit. We believed in those dreams and we never let anyone discourage us, but as we grew older those dreams began to fade and some completely disappeared. It is time you started to dream again and this time around those dreams are going to give you the energy and encouragement to get your finances on a firm foundation.

After dinner on the day I was laid off, Jon and I sat at the table and began talking about everything that happened that day. We talked about how we had lost sixty percent of our household income overnight, one of our cars, our healthcare, and the $50,000 of debt. The conversation was pretty depressing. I stopped the sad story and said to Jon, "We can't reverse what happened, so where do we go from here?" I stood up from the table and grabbed a piece of paper. I went back to the table, sat down, and wrote at the top "Dream to Reality Sheet" because I knew it was going to take some dreaming to get through the test that was in front of us.

The "Dream Sheet" helped us to figure out what we would do if money was not an issue. Where would we go, what would we do, and who would we help? The dream sheet was not where we were going to list the debt we were planning to pay off. That is not a dream. Our dreams are what we wake up for, and they are what keep us going.

We decided to separate our dreams into short, intermediate, and long term. Short term dreams were those dreams that we wanted to achieve in 6-12 months. Intermediate dreams would become reality in 3-5 years, and long term dreams would be completed in 10-15 years. The majority of the dreams would come after we paid off all of the debt. For example, in 3-5 years after paying off the debt, we wanted to save enough money to go on a two-week vacation to Europe with our entire family. An example of one of our 10-15 year dreams was to have enough money saved for college so our child or children would not have to take out student loans.

The dreams on that paper kept us out of restaurants for two-and-a-half years. They kept us out of the mall for two-and-a-half years. They kept us from going on vacation for two-and-a-half years. No one received a gift for two-and-a-half years. No gift for birthdays, Valentine's Day, anniversaries, and Christmas for Jon and me or our parents. Whenever I felt I needed a new pair of shoes I would look at the "Dream Sheet" and see that I wanted that two-week vacation to Europe more than I wanted another pair of shoes. The "Dream Sheet" was so important that I had it laminated and I placed it on the refrigerator so everyone in the house could see it. Every time we went to that refrigerator to get something out of it we would see the reasons why we were working so hard to pay the debt off.

If it has been a while since you have acknowledged your dreams or you feel that your dreams have disappeared, then it is time for you to dream again. It is time for you to say to yourself "I can have what I want most out of life." It is time for action. Create your own "Dream Sheet" like the example you see here in the back of this book. If you are not the only person in your household then everyone gets an opportunity to contribute a short term, intermediate, and long term dream to the "Dream Sheet." I don't care if you have a four-year-old child in your home. That child is allowed to have a dream on the paper. When you let children put dreams down on the "Dream Sheet" you will be surprised by what happens the next time you go to a retail store with toys. The child who put down a trip to Disneyland for their intermediate dream may ask for a toy, but when you remind them of their Disneyland dream they will want that trip more than that toy.

Even a child as young as four years old understands delayed gratification. Once all the dreams are in place on the "Dream Sheet," go to an office supply store and have it laminated. Once it is laminated, put it in an area where everyone in the household can see it. If you are the only person in your home then put the "Dream Sheet" where you can see it every day—which could still be the refrigerator or maybe it could be the mirror above the sink where you brush your teeth every day. If there is more than one person in your household then the refrigerator is the best place so that everyone is reminded everyday what their dreams are. The "Dream Sheet" should embolden you to change your financial life forever. After Jon and I finished our "Dream Sheet" I said to him "our first child was born into debt, but our second child will not be."

Debt Sucks A-ha's

1. Your "Dream Sheet" is all about what would happen in your life if money was not an issue.

2. Everyone in your household has input on the "Dream Sheet."

3. Laminate the "Dream Sheet" and put it in a visible area.

Chapter Four

What Happened to My Money?

Have you ever received your paycheck and a couple of days later you don't know where the money went? All you knew is that the money was no longer in your possession. If you feel that you always have more month than money then there is a hole in your financial boat here and you have to plug it up.

The only way to plug it up is to take the time to find out where it is. A few months after the layoff I received my W-2 statement from my former employer. I looked at how much money I brought home the previous year and the number made me sick to my stomach. Actually, what made me sick was not the number, but that I could not figure out where all the money went. What did I spend thousands of dollars on? Since this was not my first W-2 it made me wonder how much money over the years has slipped through my fingertips. When did this careless behavior of wasting money from my hard work start?

I have been working every year since I was ten years old. I started teaching tennis lessons at the age of ten and continued through college, and also worked temporary jobs at banks and restaurants when I was in high school, but there was never a time that I could remember spending all of my money. Mainly because I was still living under my parent's roof and they took care of all of my needs and even most of my wants. Since I didn't have to pay for anything it was a lot easier to save the money I was making from working different jobs. If the insanity didn't start when I was in high school or younger, then it must have started in college.

Since I was a collegiate tennis player, I never had time to work a job. In fact, whenever I applied for a job in the city where my college was located I was always denied employment because I was a tennis player. Managers thought I would not have enough time to work. It was not until my junior year of college that I was able to get a job. It was actually an eight-month internship in Minneapolis, MN.

This was not a regular internship where you go and get coffee for everyone every day, but this company paid me an annual salary of $45,000 a year, which meant that I was bringing in about $3,000 a paycheck (after taxes, etc.). Not only did they pay me, but they also provided a two-bedroom, two-bathroom apartment, a company car, and paid for the gas for all eight months. So all I used the $3K a month for was food. Let's do a little math. For eight months I was paid $3K per month which equals $24,000. When I left the internship after eight months I had $10,000. Ignoring the cost of food, that is $14K less than I should had put in my bank account.

Where did the $14K go? I only had to pay for food during the eight months and I definitely didn't eat $14K worth of food. What happened was that I was not paying attention to my spending habits, and that lack of attention cost me a lot of money. I spent money on concerts, expensive lunches, plane tickets, and who knows what else. As long as there was money in the bank and the internship check coming in each month, I felt I could spend, spend, and spend. The problem with that mentality is that I carried it into my life after college when other people no longer took care of me. I was no longer living with my parents, or on a campus being taken care of by a tennis scholarship, or in a two-bedroom, two-bath apartment paid for by an employer. I now was on my own and had to pay for my living expenses. So when I started to live on my own why didn't the spending stop? It was because I still had the perspective that as long as the money was coming in and the bills were getting paid, I was fine.

When the money stopped coming in, I knew I was not fine, and the W-2 made that feeling worse. Don't find yourself in the same position that I was in—going through life not knowing where my money was going, and then forced to pay attention because of a tragic life event. Be proactive and start to figure out how to have more money than month.

Two-Week Expense Tracking

Two weeks is all you need to begin to find out exactly where you are spending your money. You will take two weeks starting on the 1st or the 15th of the month and record all of your expenses. Why the 1st or the 15th? Those are the days that bills, especially the large bills, are due. Usually the rent, electricity, mortgage, student loan, etc., are due on the 1st or 15th. By starting on these days you will be able to account for the majority of your expenses. Whether you start on the 1st of the month or the 15th you are going to take the next two weeks to capture all the other expenses that tend to vary month-to-month—expenses such as gas, eating out, groceries, daycare, entertainment, tithing, charity, etc. If it is just you in your home then your expenses are the only ones that need to be recorded, but if you share your household with other people then everyone has to track their expenses. Parents should keep up with the expenses of children and teenagers, such as lunch money, field trip costs, school supplies, proms, extracurricular activities, etc. The goal is to record all expenses either by keeping all receipts or writing down all expenses as you spend the money. No expense is too small. If it takes a penny out of your pocket then it counts. For example, you are at the gas station and decide to go inside and buy a pack of gum for $.75; that counts as money spent and it should be recorded.

At the end of the two weeks, sit down and add up all the expenses incurred for that period of time. How much was spent on gas by everyone in the house? How much was spent on eating out or on the vending machine at work? How much does the mortgage really cost each month? Write down every expense and number. If you feel that something was left out open up past bank statements or go to your online banking and see what you may have missed.

You have found your daily and monthly expenses, but what about the money you owe? What debt do you have?

That can be found in the envelopes your creditors send to your home each month, but you may have to search deeper to make sure no debt is left out. That is where your credit report is essential. Your credit report will show all of the creditors you owe. You can find your credit report for free at AnnualCreditReport.com. You can get your credit report for free three times a year. Once from each credit bureau (Experian, Equifax, and Transunion) so make sure to get your credit report every four months.

Look at your credit report not only for your debt but also for any errors that may be on your report. During the time we were paying off our debt, I went to the Annual Credit Report website and looked at our credit report. Everything on there was familiar except one debt. It was a medical debt from college when my husband had injured his foot while playing basketball. When he went to the hospital he thought that because he was on a basketball scholarship that the university's insurance would pay for the hospital visit. He was wrong. On our credit report was a $700 debt that had been sent to collection and we knew nothing about it! We owed the money and had to add it to our list of other debts.

You cannot begin to pay off debt until you truly know what debt you have. You need to know the total amount and the monthly payment. It is time to get a game plan together and you must be ready!

Debt Sucks A-ha's

1. Look at your most recent W-2 to see how much money you really make.

2. Two week expense tracking should be done by entire household so that no expense is left out.

3. Even if one penny is spent it should be tracked!

4. Go to AnnualCreditReport.com to see what debt you owe.

Chapter Five

Game Plan

You may not have a favorite sports team. In fact, you may not like sports at all, but you have seen sports either in person or on TV at least one time while growing up. When you watched that one team or individual play that sport, how did they look? Did they look confused and chaotic? Or did they look composed and in control? More than likely they looked like they were in control of the game. The reason for that control is that they had a plan before they went out to compete. If they did not have a game plan from their coach they would lose. They would not even have a chance.

The same is true when it comes to your money. You have to have a game plan for your money so you can start winning. Up until now, because you have not had a game plan, you have continued to lose over and over again. The definition of insanity is doing the same thing over and over and expecting different results.

"How did we forget to pay this bill? Do we have the money in the bank to pay it?" These were the questions that Jon was asking me. It was pure chaos in our house when it came to our bills and our expenses. The great news was that it was the day that we were about to go over our expenses for the last two weeks. We were finally going to see where our money was going. We looked at the mortgage, we looked at how much money we were spending on gas and how much daycare cost, how much it was costing us to go out to eat, and so on. Within a few minutes, we saw why our money was disappearing so quickly. It was because we were not paying attention. It was because we didn't have a plan!

After looking at the numbers, Jon said we needed to get on a budget. That word made me cringe because I felt that I was going to be held back from life. After the anxiety faded, I decided to not call it a budget, but to call it a "spending plan." It would be my plan each month of how money would be spent.

We took the expenses for the last two weeks and started to put our first spending plan together. At the top, I put our income because knowing how much money you have coming into your household is just as important as how much money is going out. Below income I listed our expenses. By tracking the last two weeks of the expenses, it made it easier to list what we were spending our money on. I first listed our fixed expenses, such as the mortgage, the cable bill and the cell phone bill; these are the same every month. Then I listed the variable expenses, which are the expenses that differ from month to month. Gas, groceries, entertainment, and eating out are all examples of variable expenses. I only had two weeks of these expenses. In order to estimate the expense for the entire month, the numbers needed to be doubled. If $40 was spent in two weeks on gas, then $40 would be doubled to $80 for the whole month.

This process should be done for every variable expense. Once the income and expenses are listed, subtract the total expenses from the total income and see if you have money left at the end of the month or if you are losing money each month. Your spending plan will not be perfect the first month or even the fourth month, so be patient. Also, you can do your spending plan on a piece of paper each month, or if you are familiar with online banking, check with your credit union or bank to see if they have budget software.

Debt Sucks A-ha's

1. Forget budgets! Have a "spending plan" for your money.

2. Decide if the spending plan will be on paper or online.

3. Be patient. It will take time to get the spending plan right.

Chapter Six

Something Has to Go

When I saw the final number after I subtracted our expenses from our income, I knew a change was coming. This change would have to do with what our monthly expenses would be going forward. At this time, we were surviving on my husband's income and my unemployment income, which was close to nothing. I knew that even when I found a full-time job again, we were not going to be able to keep spending the same amount of money and also pay off the $50,000 of debt. The math didn't work!

When you look at your spending plan, does your math work? If it doesn't, there is a fun game that I would like you to play. It is called the "Something Has to Go" game. This is a game that everyone hates to play, but in order to make progress in paying off debt, some thing or some things on your spending plan have to go! They don't have to go six months or a year from now, but they have to go today!

When I saw the reasons that we were experiencing more month than money, I took a deep look at the spending plan to see what could be eliminated or reduced. I didn't make the decisions alone, but Jon and I made them together. We had to open up bill statements to see if we could adjust certain expenses, and as a result keep some money in our bank accounts each month. The cell phone bills were first. I looked at both bills to see how many minutes were used as well as data. Turns out we were not using all the data we were paying for, so that is what was cut out first. By reducing the cell phone plans, our household was able to save $50 a month. After the cell phone bill, I opened up the cable bill because we had every channel the cable company offered, so I knew there had to be savings in cutting back on it. I love watching TV, but even I had to admit there was not enough time in a lifetime to watch all of those channels. Cutting back on cable helped us save $80. After seeing the savings from those two bills, it made me motivated to find even more savings. We eliminated gym and magazine memberships, as well as newspaper subscriptions. The most surprising savings I found was when I sat down with our insurance agent and reevaluated our home and auto insurance. We saved a nice amount of money monthly by changing our coverage. We went line after line of the spending plan to see what could be eliminated or at least decreased.

Look at your completed spending plan and see what has to go. There should be multiple expenses that can be cut back. The expense that usually costs households the most is dining out. This expense is separate from groceries, and it involves all types of eating out. Dining out at an expensive restaurant as well as a restaurant with value meals can cost you big time each month. Eating out was costing us $200 a month, because I was a new mom who was too tired to cook. As a result, we ate out at least three times a week. We didn't go to expensive sit-down restaurants, but we would go to restaurants with the value menu. Two people eating off the value menu three times or more a week will add up! Earlier in the book, I told you that we did not go out to eat for two and a half years, but that didn't save us $200 a month, but instead $150 because we had to add $50 to the existing grocery expense so that we could cook more. When you cut back on dining out, remember that you will need more groceries.

There are other expenses that are a little trickier to cut. The electric and water bill never can go completely away, so you have to be clever in order to see savings. Savings on electricity is all in the thermometer. During the spring, when the temperature starts to rise, is the time to turn the heat completely off until it gets closer to the summer. When the summer temperatures rise high enough, air conditioning can come on. When the fall season arrives and the heat starts to fade, that is the time to cut the air conditioning off until it gets too cold that the heat has to come back on. This will help you save hundreds on your energy bill each year.

No Spending Days

While you are in the mood of eliminating, it is time to figure out which days of the week are going to be your "no spending days." "No spending days" are the days of the week that you will spend no money. You will not buy gas, food, clothes, or anything! Pick at least two days to start with and if you can handle more than two days, then do it! Once you pick the two days or more, those are your "no spending days" from now on!

Debt Sucks A-ha's

1. Start making a list of expenses that have to go.

2. Call the companies of those expenses and discontinue service.

3. Pick two or more "no spending days" and stick to them!

Chapter Seven

Never Pay Full Price Again

I have a saying, "If it is free, it is for me!" In all seriousness, you may not be able to get everything for free, but you can get a majority of items for a discount. By this point you have cut a lot out from your spending plan. It is now time to see how you can stop paying full price for the expenses you have left.

Did you leave entertainment in your spending plan? Maybe you want to go to the movies every now and then. If movies are what you enjoy, there is an inexpensive way to see movies. You can go to a Redbox location and rent a movie for $1. Or you can wait until Redbox sends you a code for a free movie rental. You also can go to your local library and rent numerous movies for free. All you need is a library card.

The library is also a wonderful place for more than just checking out books. You can read numerous magazines and newspapers for free while at the library. There are some libraries that have partnerships with companies like Zinio, which allows people with a library card to download magazines and music for free. The bottom line is before you spend money on entertainment, go to your local library.

While Jon and I were in debt, our favorite thing to do was to eat out. We would go to new restaurants in town to try new food all the time. If we didn't feel like cooking, we would go and pick up a value meal. We didn't need a major excuse to spend money on eating out. "I'm tired. Let's just eat out tonight." "I had a bad day at work. Let's go to a restaurant and talk about it." "It's cold outside. Let's go to a restaurant and get a hot meal." The smallest reason would have us spending our hard earned money. When we decided not to dine out anymore until the debt was paid off, I think that decision hurt me the most! Jon would go out to eat with me, but really it didn't matter if we ate out or at home. I was the one who loved trying new foods and new restaurants, so the thought of not being able to do that for a while gave me some anxiety. The thought of all the future restaurants that would come to the city and I would not be able to experience them made me sad.

I decided that I would find another way for us to go out to dinner, but to go out to dinner for free! I started reading the free local papers and magazines that you find in grocery stores and in doctors' offices. I found that in these magazines, they listed local events that would be happening around the city each month. A majority of the events were free and open to the public. One day as I was looking through one of the magazines, I came across a free healthy cooking class. It was being sponsored by the local hospital in partnership with the YWCA. I signed Jon and myself up to attend the class because it was an opportunity to do something together without spending money. This class more than surpassed my expectations. I thought we were going to watch someone cook a dish and then we would get samples to try, but I was completely wrong!

When we arrived to the cooking class, we were put into groups of two, which was perfect because Jon and I came together. We were given our own ingredients from the recipe as well as a stove to cook on. The instructor walked us through the cooking steps and gave us ways to eat healthier. Once the food was finished, the class sat down to eat the food that was cooked. All of this was great, but it wasn't the best part. The best part was that before we left the class, we were given more ingredients, including meat to take home with us so that we could recreate the meal! All of this fun was FREE! The class was offered twice a month, so Jon and I used it as our date night and we were able to enjoy free meals that were also healthy.

Since we are talking about food, groceries is an expense that you can easily save on. Groceries can never be cut out because everyone has to eat, so if you have to spend your life paying, you need to find ways to save. The easiest way to save on groceries is to sign up for the rewards program at your local grocery store. Grocery stores always give savings to their rewards program members. Make sure to sign up on their email list so that you know when items go on sale. Being in the program means instant savings without the use of coupons. There have been many trips to the grocery store that I have saved $50 or more because of the rewards program!

Coupons will bring you even more savings and you don't have to be a coupon expert. You just need to be aware of what products you buy at the grocery store on a regular basis and look for coupons that will help you save on those products. There is no need to buy a newspaper every Sunday to get the coupons out of it. There are websites like mysavings.com that have various types of coupons, and sometimes you can print multiple copies of the same coupon. That means even more savings for you!

Clothes are another item that you cannot go without. Up until this point, you may have been into name brand clothes, but those designer labels have cost you a lot of money. I was part of the crowd who always had to have name brand clothes. I wasted too much money on clothes that probably cost the company it came from pennies to make. Our household did not buy any clothes during the time we were getting out of debt. The only person that was exempt was my one-year-old son, J.R., who was growing every week! While buying clothes for him, I learned how to save money on clothes throughout the year.

When I shopped for clothes, I realized that there were clothes always on sale. The clothes would usually be the clothes that were out of season or soon-to-be out of season. For example, in September, I was shopping for some long-sleeve shirts for J.R. As I was walking around the store, I saw that the summer clothing was 50-70% off. It didn't matter if it was short-sleeve shirts, shorts, or swim trunks; all of it was deeply discounted. Then I had an epiphany! All the clothes that were going out of season were discounted because the store needed to get rid of the merchandise. They would not be selling these summer clothes next summer, so they had to go. The same thing happened during the springtime when all the winter clothes went on sale. These types of sales were not unique to this store, but every retailer does this, including thrift stores where clothes are already discounted! Always make sure to shop out of season so that you never pay full price for clothing. To this day I buy children clothes this way. I make sure I always buy the size that I think the child will be in the following season. It doesn't matter the size or the age, you can always save money by buying out of season.

Debt Sucks A-ha's

1. If you didn't cut certain expenses out, your goal is to find a way not to pay full price for that expense.

2. Look locally for ways to entertain yourself or your family for free.

3. Join the rewards program at local grocery stores.

4. Start to search for off-season clothes and see how much money you can save.

Chapter Eight

I Need More Money

You have cut your spending plan to the bare minimum of expenses, but you find that there is still not enough extra money each month to really make a dent in your debt. That is a sign that you have to bring more money in, but how? This is where you have to get creative, and once your creative juices start flowing, you will find all types of ways to make the money flow into your household.

After two months of working our spending plan, I could see that we were saving about $300 a month, but $300 a month was not going to get $50,000 of debt paid off quickly. We needed to do more, much more! I've always been a person who sold stuff to other people. Ever since I was a little girl, I knew how to separate people from their money. When I was seven years old, someone taught me a game that involved taking coins from people's hands. The game went like this: I would ask a person, usually an adult, if they had a coin. Most of the time, I would ask if they had a quarter, but if they didn't, I would ask if they had a nickel or a dime. When they pulled the coin out of their pocket, I would tell them that I could take the coin out the palm of their hand. The trick was that I would put the back of my hand on top of their palm and the coin. All they had to do was close their hand before I turned my hand around to grab it. Everyone that I played this trick on never could believe that this little seven-year-old would be able to turn her hand around in time to snatch the coin out.

I snatched the coin out every time, and my bank account began to fill up! I would do the trick on every adult during family get-togethers, at school on my friends, and pretty much anywhere! Most of the time I would trick the same person multiple times because they would keep taking coins out of their pocket to see if they could beat me. It never happened. I would use the money to buy candy, snacks, and small toys. It was a great business.

That was a magic trick that I used to get money, but as I grew up I would sell candy to neighborhood children, unwanted jewelry and clothes to friends in high school, and snacks to roommates and student athletes in college. Even my career after college was in selling, so it is definitely in my blood and it was time that I tapped into that skill to bring more money into our household.

One Saturday, I started to walk around the house to see what could be sold. The first item I found in our closet was a microwave that was still in the box that we received as a wedding present two years earlier. We had never opened it, and once we moved into the house, there was already a microwave installed, so we didn't need it. I took the microwave out of the closet, loaded it in the back of the car and headed to the nearest pawn shop. The pawn shop gave me $40 for the microwave, and I was super excited! Forty bucks may seem like a small number, but when you think that it was for a microwave collecting dust, then that $40 looks a lot better! That small victory motivated me to find even more items to sell.

I started walking around the house again on that same Saturday, and as I walked room to room, there was something that most of the rooms had in common: TVs! We had five TVs for two and a half people, the half being our toddler son. I talked to Jon and convinced him that we didn't need five TVs and we should sell them. The following Saturday, we loaded three of the five TVs and took them to three different pawn shops and sold them. Why three different pawn shops? Pawn shops are in the business of loaning you money by holding onto your item, and they expect you to come back and give them money to get it back from them. If they know you are not coming back to get the item, they will give you less money. The average amount of money we received from each TV was in the range of $60-80! Those TVs gave us a quick $200, and when you combine that money with the $40 from the microwave and the $300 from the spending plan cuts, that is over $500 that month that went to paying off the debt!

Clothes are another money maker and you can sell them in different ways. You can sell them on eBay or take them to thrift stores. The easiest way to clean out your closet and make money off the clothes is to have yard sales. We had yard sales every Saturday the first summer after my layoff. We spent the entire winter before gathering clothing, shoes, and everything else in our house that we no longer wanted and stacked all of it into one room until the hot weather arrived. Once the summer arrived, I put the yard sale sign out in the grass during the week. That

Saturday we put all the items outside our garage at 7AM and began to sell. The first weekend we made $200 in four hours! What a great feeling knowing that all we did was sit there and talk to people and we made $200. If we didn't sell everything, which we didn't, we would put what was left back out the next Saturday along with other items we found in the house. One week would make $300 and another week $450. The best weekend we had we made $800 because we sold our lawn mower. Yard sales helped us bring in $1500 or more during the month and that helped a lot towards the paying down of the debt.

You may not live in the best place for a yard sale, but you should know someone who lives in an area that will allow you to have a yard sale. Ask that person if they would mind if you set up your items at their home. If they seem a little reluctant, tell them that you will give them five percent of your sales. Do not go above ten percent. If you make $200 in a few hours, you give them $20 for the work they didn't do and tell them you will see them next week.

Part-time jobs are another way to earn money. Part-time jobs don't have to be so difficult that you work an extra thirty hours in addition to your current forty hours. It could be as little as ten hours a week. The point is to earn extra money that can be used to pay down your debt. Part-time jobs can be "work at home" jobs where you can work on the weekends or during your free time. It can be a part-time job outside of your home, like a receptionist at a gym on the weekend or bookkeeping for a small business.

Hobbies are activities that we enjoy doing. We enjoy them so much that we would do them for free. If professional athletes never had the ability to be paid for what they do they would still play their favorite sport. The same with people who love the work they do on a daily basis. We love our hobbies and we do them for free. The best part about hobbies is that we are really good at whatever our hobby is. There are people who love to sew, and if you see the items that they have created you would see immediately how talented they are in the sewing department. There are other people who can sing very well and have participated in songs in church all of their lives. They have sung the national anthem one hundred times in front of a crowd.

When you have a hobby or talent that you are recognized for over and over by other people, it may be a hobby you can be paid to do. As you already know, I grew up playing tennis and Jon grew up playing basketball. After college was over both of these sports became our hobbies and we only played when we had time and energy. Although we didn't practice twice a day like we did when we were in college, we still could best the majority of people who challenged us. We used our talent in these sports to make some money. We did this instead of looking for a traditional part-time job.

We made money with both sports by training young people who were in middle school and high school. We had been to college on athletic scholarships and knew what it took to get there. I would charge $25 an hour for a tennis lesson and Jon would charge $30 or more per kid per basketball lesson. Jon would always make more money because he could have five basketball players in one hour-long session which meant he could make $150 for one hour of work. I did tennis lessons as long as it was warm outside, and he did his basketball training year round. This was easy money for us because we loved tennis and basketball.

What do you love to do that would enable you to make money? If you are drawing a blank and truly can't come up with anything then go to your friends and family and ask what they think you are good at. Maybe you are a teacher who is good at a particular subject. You could make money by tutoring children or college students. Do you enjoy cutting grass and find yourself cutting other people's grass for free? Maybe it is time to start finding paying customers. Do you enjoy taking pictures? I am sure there are some people in your community that would love to pay you to take engagement photos, family photos, or just pictures at a local event. Whatever your hobby is, whatever your passion may be, turn it into earning an income.

Debt Sucks A-ha's

1. If you need to bring in more money start looking for items around the house to sell.

2. Decide where those items will be sold. Ex: eBay, yard sale, pawn shop, etc.

3. Decide what hobbies you enjoy and how you could earn an income from them.

Chapter Nine

Passion to Profit

So many companies have been created by someone following their passion. Yes, it takes more than passion to have a successful company, but passion is what lies at the beginning. I want to share a few companies that I know of that were started with a passion in mind and have grown into companies with international recognition. I picked each company because I am impressed by the owners, their company, and their hard work to make their company a success!

The first company is Cynfull Sweets and I have known the owner Cyntrina Montgomery for almost twenty years. I have seen her take her passion for baking to the next level with Cynfull Sweets. I would drive the five hours just for her delicious red velvet cupcakes! Here is her story in her words.

Cynfull Sweets became official in 2012 when I decided to step out on faith and turn my hobby into a career. I have been baking since I was 9 years old and mainly it was because I have a serious sweet tooth. As I got older I enjoyed baking for others who loved desserts as much as I did. It wasn't until college when I started getting orders around the Thanksgiving and Christmas holidays where people were offering to pay. I initially only wanted the money for pocket change and really didn't think much more of it.

I moved to Atlanta in 2007 where the demand for orders increased. It wasn't just holidays anymore, there were requests at potlucks, birthdays, kid's birthday parties, and wedding showers. During this same time my corporate job as a paralegal no longer satisfied me and I enrolled in graduate school to earn my Master's Degree in hopes that I can secure a higher paid position at my current place of employment or elsewhere. I graduated in 2013 with honors and I began applying for new positions. I must have applied to hundreds of positions for almost 2 years and only received one call back and interview where I didn't get the position. I was so confused and I kept asking God why can't I get ahead?! I have debt I want to pay off, I want to buy a house, and I want to restart my savings and I just knew a higher paid position was the answer. Wrong!

One day, I was scrolling through Facebook and I saw a graphic that basically stated that you won't get ahead and get more blessings until you appreciate and do right by your current blessings. This made me realize why God had not blessed me with a higher paid position. I didn't get a higher paid position because I already made enough money to pay down my debt, buy a home, and start saving. I needed to be better disciplined with my current salary so I could achieve my goals. What sense would it make for me to make more money if my habits haven't changed? None!

I would just be in the same mess a year later. I also realized that the positions I applied for I was not truly interested in. My goal was the salary listed. So, I typed out some financial goals to achieve and I started making some serious changes on how I managed my money. Once I started changing my financial habits I was promoted at my job making more money!

My passion is baking and I realized and thank God for every time I was in a financial bind or on the verge of being in a financial bind, I would suddenly get a bakery order. I know that it was God showing me he had my back and that I just need to have faith in him.

So, it's 2016 and I am working on expanding Cynfull Sweets into the wedding industry. Weddings are money makers and I love love! I have ideas and plans in mind that I am working on having as a reality by Wedding Season 2017. My plan is to do a soft launch fall 2016 and the overall goal is to leave my corporate job and fully go into business for myself. This passion drives me to become a better baker, cake decorator, and overall successful entrepreneur. There are some falls along the way but there is only failure if I give up. My plan is to retire as a baker.

Facebook: Cynfull Sweets

Twitter: @CynfullSweets

Instagram: @cynfullsweets.

Website at www.cynfullsweets.com

The next company Sweet Visions loves bringing smiles to people's faces with their sweet treats! The owner Alexa Edwards unique decorations and style keeps her customers coming back for more! Here is how Sweet Visions became a reality!

After watching a YouTube video, I made my first batch of cake pops for my family Christmas Day 2010. Visually they didn't look so appealing but they tasted great and became the talk of the party. By the time Valentine's Day 2011 rolled around the word had spread about these cake pops and I ended up with 14 orders to fill for family and friends. Sweet Visions was born and over the past six years has grown, evolved, and most importantly taught me countless lessons about entrepreneurship.

The journey toward building a brand and products that I'm proud of has been one of the most rewarding experiences for me to date. I am an educational psychologist by training and have spent most of my adult life conducting research on academic issues affecting students. While this work has been fulfilling in many ways it leaves little room for me to explore the creative side of my personal passion.

"Each of us has a personal calling that's as unique as a fingerprint and the best way to succeed is to discover what you love and then find a way to offer it to others...."Oprah Winfrey

It just so happens that "MY" love is creating customized sweets that help people celebrate special moments and events in their lives. Nothing gives more satisfaction than seeing the look on a client's face when they see a box of treats and goodies made especially for them.

What started as a cake pop venture has now turned into a full offering of treats including cupcakes, rice Krispy treat pops, dipped oreos, gourmet strawberries, candy apples, and more. Our customer base or "Sweet Fans" as we call them has grown tremendously and we look forward to more continued SWEET success in the future!

Sweet Visions

FB: https://www.facebook.com/visionarysweets

Instagram: @Visionary_Sweets

Periscope: @SweetVisions

All businesses do not have to strive for an international presence. There are millions of businesses that have a goal of serving their community and their city as a whole. This next business does exactly that! Greater Vision Child Care is a place where tomorrow's leaders are being taught today! Its' owner Kenya Heck has a passion for teaching children and showing those children how to be the best they can be!

I was working a sit-down job all day and it was so boring. I thought to myself there has to be something else for me do. So I kept working and saving money and one day as I was sitting at my desk and I heard childcare and I said no way God I just bought my house and set it up perfect just for me. That night during prayer I heard it again so I thought to myself wow! The next day at my desk I started writing down what I seen and the name Greater Vision

Child Care appeared. The name was perfect because surely the vision was greater than me!

As of today I have a successful Child care and I wouldn't change it for the world. Seven years and counting and I'm believing God for Greater! Greater Vision Child Care is a four star facility and currently serves 14 families! In the future we are trying expand to serve more families to impact the community! Teaching and caring for children is my passion and that passion has led to a successful business!

The next two businesses are really unique and before I learned of them I had never seen anything like it before! Food trucks are currently a big rave and these trucks that serve different types of cuisine are all over the United States. Food trucks have become so popular that there are tv shows about how to start your own food truck empire. The next two businesses are on a truck and a bus, but they don't serve food. What they offer is much more exciting!

The Pink Culture Truck is owned by Meka Harrell and it is the first pink fashion truck that I have ever seen! Her clothing and accessories are fashion forward and she has customers all over the country and I'm sure the world as well! She shares where her love for fashion started.

Born and raised in Baltimore, Maryland, I started my love for fashion at the young age of 16. I spent those days working at my God father's clothing store (DaDa's), where I worked paycheck to paycheck for the latest fashion trends that the store offered. Eventually my family and I moved to North Carolina, where I attended

Livingstone College, making me the first person in my family to obtain a college degree. While working a 9-5 in the health care industry, I came up with the idea of moving back home to Baltimore to start my very own boutique. Somehow that plan was postponed and I decided to obtain my MBA and attended Pfeiffer University in 2008.

Upon graduation, my entrepreneurial fire was lit and I came up with Pink Culture. Though it wasn't until 5 years later, Pink Culture finally came to life via the Fashion Truck Industry. August 8, 2013, was the official opening of Pink Culture Mobile Boutique. Pink Culture and I have literally been on a roll since opening. I have spoken about "Stepping Out on Faith" at several school engagements from middle, high school and college level. Pink Culture has been rolling anywhere from Charlotte to Raleigh for food truck events, Homecoming Experiences and some amazing festivals in NC. You can even attend some of the cool events hosted by Pink Culture, such as fashion shows, crafting parties or read a few pages in my first Ebook "Confessions of a Mobile Fashionista".

If I am not on the truck, speaking, or planning events I am with my family. My number one priority is family and I truly enjoy spending time with my husband, and three children. I am extremely excited about the future and growth of Pink Culture. Be sure to follow the journey on twitter and Instagram @PinkCultrTruck for all things fashion truck and @PinkCulture for the Brand experience and remember if you see the truck to #Honkifurafashionista

Website: www.pinkculturetruck.com

Instagram: @PinkCultrTruck, @PinkCulture

The next business is not a truck, but a bus! Its' founder Marsha Barnes, a certified financial educator and personal finance expert has the same passion that I have, personal finance! I love her business and how she helps people with their finances. She is the first ever mobile financial hub and she is helping people one mile at a time! Here is her story in her words.

I recognized that there was an incredible buzz around our nation on the topic of personal finance. No longer did it become necessary to seek out the local financial planner, or accountant for information that could lead to a healthy financial lifestyle. You can easily find blogs on personal finance, money coaches and even in the news finance is strategically inserted into segments. However, what you can't find is face to face accessibility at many of the locations where you spend most of your time. The Finance Bar was derived from the vision that most Americans spent 9-12 hours in the workplace, some are consumed at the organizations that they lead or are a part of a great percentage of their time, and there's no secret that financial literacy is missing from most college campuses.

The Finance Bar mobile hub fills those gaps by offering on-site personal finance teachings to corporations, organizations and educational institutions. However, the fun doesn't stop there. The Finance Bar also offers a virtual Members Club for women who are committed to transforming their financial lifestyle. With the understanding that many seek accountability, The Finance Bar Members Club provides members with 24-7 access to a virtual hub where they can find a plethora of information and guided exercises that are led by nationally recognized personal finance experts. There's also a mobile app that provides real time access to how much should be spent on expenses based on your individual income available for Apple and Android users.

You can learn more about The Finance Bar by visiting www.thefinancebar.com.

Facebook: @thefinancebar

Twitter: @thefinancebar

Instagram: @thefinancebar

Pintrest: @thefinancebar

Last, but not least is Chisa D. Pennix-Brown, MBA and she is the owner of Lady Bizness. She goes by Lady Bizness and she helps businesses to grow and reach higher levels! She is able to look at any business and map out a plan for their success. What is so awesome about Lady Bizness herself and the company she runs is that she only needs a computer to operate. She can be in Sydney, Australia and working with a business in Milan, Italy! Her location does not determine who she does business with on a daily basis! Here is how her journey began!

I am unapologetically an Entrepreneur. That means I have a million ideas, I'm always thinking about my business and how I can improve it. My name is Chisa D. Pennix-Brown, MBA and I am the CEO of Lady Bizness. My company is a part of my DNA and has taken years to develop into a brand that is recognized for quality. That was one of the biggest goals I set for myself when I came up with the idea for a company whose purpose lies in helping others reach their goals of business ownership.

Lady Bizness has transitioned several times since I graduated from Elon University in 2001. I always knew I wanted my own company and that I wanted to be in control of earning more than corporate America wanted to offer. The only way to dictate your worth is to evolve and work hard. I have fired myself and reinvented from C Phoenix Marketing, to Phoenix Brown, and finally settled on Lady Bizness in 2010. The nine years between graduation and incorporation showed me what adjustments I needed to make to ensure success. The number one constant in business is always money. I had to break up with the idea that breaking even was good. I had to truly evaluate having all the bells and whistles. I had to change my methodology from being seen at everything. Money truly shaped the way that I made choices when I looked at how much work went into an event or a client. I took a long look at what I could do better and how to improve efficiency.

Once I realized how much I really wanted to make then I had to find a way to garner the attention of those that could afford my rates. This was a pivotal change because I had to stop a lot of negative things that kept my finances from flourishing. I started a practice that I call the 90 Day Focus. This process has become a way of life for me and those that follow the path to achieving goals.

The 90 day focus says that you can choose one personal and one professional goal and work 90 minutes a day for 90 consecutive days to achieve it. Therefore, behaviors and activities, no matter how tempting, that do not fall in line with those goals have to be eliminated. This mindset change has been the most important thing for my business. Focus on one business goal for 90 days and do the activities necessary for you to get what you need. Money is not the most important thing in life, but it does allow you to live the life you want, and that for me, includes having a thriving business. If you can be a good steward of your finances, provide great quality, and excellent service you will create a #ShowUpandShowOut business.

Website: LadyBizness.com
Facebook: @LadyBizness
Twitter: @LadyBizness
Instagram: @LadyBizness
Periscope: @LadyBizness

Chapter Ten

"In Case You Are Breathing" Fund

Did you just feel your chest go up and then back down? That is called breathing and it means you are alive! Every day you are breathing you must recognize that you have to be prepared for financial emergencies. The majority of people could not come up with $2000 if an emergency came up. There are a lot of people who could not even come up with $500 if something went wrong. When you are not prepared then you can find yourself falling back into debt and it becomes an endless cycle that can last your entire life.

The "In Case You Are Breathing Fund" (ICYABF) is your safety net for emergencies. The ICYABF will help you pay off debt quicker because you won't borrow more money in order to pay off your debts. Your ICYABF should have at least $500 in it to start off and that will take care of minor emergencies, like a flat tire or the cost of a plumber. $500 is just the start. It would be best to have $1500 or $2000 in your ICYABF because there are big expenses that can cost that amount of money. If your water heater breaks down that could cost more than $1000. Unexpected medical bills can cost in the thousands. An ICYABF will make sure you do not go into panic mode every time an emergency happens. Panic mode causes you to become desperate and will lead you to borrow money that you don't have to borrow. Think about the last time you had an emergency and how you couldn't think with a clear mind. Maybe the air conditioner in your car stopped working in the middle of the summer and everyday was a high of ninety six- degrees. Heat and sweat will make you think you can't survive and you need another car, and not just another car, but you need the $20,000 new car that you just saw on TV!

Your ICYABF will need to be funded at the same time you make your debt payments. Once you have put $1500 or $2000 in your ICYABF you will have a cushion such that you can aggressively attack your debt. If you run into an emergency and have to use some of the ICYABF then you will need to reimburse your ICYABF before returning to aggressively paying your debt down. For example your car needs $500 in repairs and that brings your ICYABF down from $2000 to $1500. You will need to pause aggressively paying down your debt until you replenish the fund with $500 to take it back up to $2000. Of course, all of this assumes that you continue to make your normal monthly debt payments.

You may be thinking how am I going to come up with $1500 dollars or $2000 dollars? The reason that I waited to talk about ICYABF is because I first wanted to make sure you knew where your money was going by following the two-week expense tracking. I also wanted you to be able to save money monthly by cutting out expenses and bring more money in by selling items and monetizing your hobbies. If you do these things, then hopefully you will have extra money every month, and that extra money should be used to build your ICYABF.

There are other ways to quickly put money in your ICYABF. Tax refunds are definitely a quick way to build your fund. Think back over the years how much you have received in tax refunds. Most people receive a couple thousand dollars, if not more. Use your next tax refund to get the $2000 in your ICYABF that you need, and if there is any money left put it towards paying down your debt. If you work for a company that gives bonuses or raises, then that is another opportunity to build up your ICYABF. Bonuses may come once a year or multiple times a year, but whenever you do get a bonus put all of that extra money into your fund. Raises are not as often so when you do get a raise you have to be smart with it. If you have been making it fine on your current paycheck then when the raise goes into effect pretend that you still get paid the same amount before the raise. Use the money from the raise to fund your ICYABF, even if it's $50 a month. That $50 can go a long way!

When you start saving for your ICYABF you need to put the money in a place that is safe (and that safe place is not your sock drawer). It needs to be placed in a location where it is hard for you to get access to it. A bank or a credit union is where your ICYABF should go because these institutions can put extra layers of security in place that will make it hard for you just to withdraw the money. You don't want it to be easy to take the money out because you will never be able to fully fund your ICYABF and that will keep you in a cycle of going back into debt every time an emergency comes around. Make sure to find financial institutions that will give you a free savings account or at least one that only costs $5 to open and that $5 will go into your savings account.

Your ICYABF should not stop at $2000. That is just the beginning. When you pay all of your debt off your ICYABF needs to be funded in an amount that would cover a year's worth of living expenses. For example, if your monthly expenses are $3000 then your fully funded ICYABF should be $3000 multiplied by twelve months, which equals $36,000. You may be wondering why you need enough money saved to cover a year's worth of expenses. The reason for the amount is that many people, including myself, have found that job security does not exist anymore and at any time a company can decide that your services are no longer needed. If that happens, you are in a much better position financially if you have a year's worth of expenses covered by savings in a bank or credit union. Having a year of expenses covered will give you time to find the right career with the pay that you want. If you don't have enough money saved then you become desperate and that desperation can show itself in a job interview. The interviewer will sense the desperation and offer you less pay and fewer benefits, or not hire you at all. Your ICYABF protects you from other people who want to take advantage of you, and helps to prevent or reduce feelings of desperation.

Debt Sucks A-ha's

1. Think back on the past emergencies you experienced and the stress it caused you. How would you have felt if you had the money in the bank to pay for that emergency?

2. The ICYABF is to be at least $500, but the goal should be to get it up to $2000.

3. Make sure to put your ICYABF in a financial institution and put restraints in place so that it is not easy for you to withdraw the money.

4. Once you pay off all of your debt build your ICYABF with enough savings to cover a year's worth of living expenses.

Chapter Eleven

The Power of NO!

None of the information set forth in this book will work if you don't know how to say one word. You have to have the courage to say this word as many times as it is needed. That word is NO! You may feel that you have no problem saying the word "no," but the truth is most of the debt we find ourselves in is because of our inability to say "no." The majority of the money we spend is because we can't say that simple word. You have to be able to say "no" to friends, family, strangers, and most importantly, yourself!

I loved hanging with my friends especially in college and after college. That hanging out used to be free hangouts, but once we started making money, either from part time jobs or our careers, those hang outs became hangouts with receipts. Friends don't make you spend a lot of money all at one time. Friends usually cause you to spend small amounts of money over and over again and that is what usually ends up costing you half your annual salary. Friends are able to appeal to your emotions and lead you towards retail therapy. Retail therapy is when you spend money to make yourself feel better about a situation that may have upset you. Your friends will be able to get you to spend $30 on a manicure or $60 on a new outfit because you had a bad day at work. Friends will convince you that you deserve to go on an $800 island vacation because you have worked so hard for the past six months. The spa treatments, dinners out, vacations, etc., will cost you thousands of dollars every year. Thousands of dollars that could have gone to paying off debt. Thousands of dollars that could have gone to your ICYABF or retirement. While you are going through this "debt sucks" process you will have to let your friends know that you are trying to improve your financial future. You won't be able to go out to dinner all the time or go on that yearly trip. When you feel yourself getting weak just look at your "Dream Sheet" and remember what you really want. Also remember true friends want to see you happy and they will understand that your happiness lies in reaching a place in your life where you no longer have to worry about your finances.

Family is much harder to say no to because they are blood and we have known them all of our lives. They have raised us and given us life-changing advice, which creates an emotional feeling of indebtedness to them. The problem with this feeling is that if you are in debt and have a problem saying "no" to family members your financial situation will get worse. You will go into more debt trying to help family out.

The biggest mistake I see people make when it comes to their family is co-signing. College loans, payday loans, business loans, car loans, apartment leases, even mortgages. There is a reason that banks want a co-signor. It is because the bank knows that the person you are co-signing for may not be able to pay the bill. They need someone, and that someone will be you, to pay the bill when it becomes past due. When you start receiving calls from the bank and eventually debt collectors you will see the importance of the word "no." You are the one who gets hurt the most when you co-sign. You become upset every time you see the person you co-signed for spending money or not answering your phone calls. Your credit score gets trashed unless you spend your hard earned money to keep the payments current. The worst part is that the person you co-signed for who is not answering your call is still driving that car, living in that home or apartment, etc.

Another opportunity to say "no" to family is when they want to borrow money. The issue with letting family members borrow money is that it probably won't be the last time. Once they know they can come to you and borrow money you may become their new bank. If you are a multimillionaire then maybe you can be a "bank" to someone, but if you are trying to pay off debt you really can't afford to let family members or anyone else borrow money.

Strangers are a lot easier to say "no" to because, let's be real, you don't really know them. The problem comes when that stranger has something you want and that stranger has amazing selling skills. The strangers that have the best chance to separate you from your hard-earned are the credit card companies. They are everywhere. They are on the TV, they are on the radio, they are in the airports, and on the flight. Credit card companies use enticing language, such as free flights, cash back, and earned points.

What the credit card companies don't tell you is that it is a trillion-dollar industry and that in 2014 $4 trillion dollars were processed on credit cards. Where does all that money come from? It comes from people with the credit cards. Although there were $4 trillion dollars processed there was still $712 billion of credit card debt that was not paid by the end of that year. Who was in possession of that debt? It was not the credit card company, it was people like you and me—people who are trying to make their lives better financially.

I have not always said "no" to credit card companies. Once when I was in a store shopping for more clothes that I didn't need, I ran into a situation that millions of shoppers run into every day. As I was putting my clothes down on the counter to pay for them the saleswoman asked "Would you like to save twenty percent by opening a credit card?" All I heard the saleswoman say was "twenty percent" and I was filling out the paperwork. Whenever people sign up for a store credit card for the first time if they have never had a credit card before, many times they really don't know what they are doing, and that was definitely the case for me.

After I signed up for the credit card it was immediately obvious that I was absolutely clueless about credit cards and how they work. I actually tried to pay for the clothing that day with my debit card and, of course, the saleswoman had to educate me about my new credit card. She said "Put that away. The bill will come in the mail and you can pay for it then." The confused look on my face soon turned to worry as I realized I was over my head. Right then and there I should have had the courage to tell her to tear up the application. I didn't have the courage and because I didn't have that courage, I deserved what happened next.

Since I had the clothes I completely forgot about paying for them. I saw the bill when it arrived, but with the craziness of everyday life I completely forgot to pay it until it was almost too late. At the last minute I put cash money in an envelope and sent it to the company. I felt a big relief that I didn't miss the deadline for payment. About two weeks went by and I received mail from the credit card company. I thought maybe they were sending me a "thank you" letter for paying on time. Yeah right! The credit card company had sent me another bill with the same amount that I had already paid two weeks earlier, and this time it had a late fee attached.

I stayed calm because obviously the credit card company had made a mistake and I would just call the customer service so they could fix it. When the customer service representative answered the phone I explained how I paid the bill and that I did not owe any money. The representative asked for my full name and began to search the system for the payment. After a few minutes the representative came back and said the payment could not be found. At this point I was starting to become impatient because I felt the credit card company was trying to cheat me out of my money.

I told the representative that I had personally put actual cash into an envelope and sent the envelope off in time. What the representative said next infuriated me. "Mam, you are never supposed to put actual money in an envelope. People at the post office probably stole your money or people here stole it." I was so angry that I had to pay for those clothes twice that I hung up the phone, went to my purse to get the credit card, and put it in the shredder. You may be thinking that was so dumb. The credit card company would never get the best of me. As you are convincing yourself of that think of this one statistic. Households in America have an average credit card debt of $15,355. Imagine the amount of debt you are in now and then add $15,355 on top of that. That is the danger you put yourself in by keeping credit cards in your possession, so it is best to stay away from credit cards altogether.

There is no one that is going to get more money out of you than YOU! The hardest person to say "no" to is yourself. You can make the best arguments in your head about why you should spend money. You will convince yourself that you need a new car, even though your current car runs fine. You will tell yourself that you have lived in an apartment long enough and that you need a five-bedroom house for only you and your spouse. You will go on vacations on a credit card because "you deserve it," and you tell yourself you will pay it off in a few months. Saying "no" and having the discipline to stick to your decision is what will keep you from making the biggest financial mistakes of your life.

With so many people after your money, start today practicing saying the word "NO." Start saying "no" to your friends, family, strangers, and definitely yourself. The more you say "no" the more money you will have to pay off debt and to save. The more money you will have to make the dreams on your Dream Sheet a reality.

Debt Sucks A-ha's

1. Telling friends about your journey to be free of debt will keep them from pressuring you to spend money.

2. Never co-sign for anyone because if they can't pay the bill, you will be forced to pay it for them.

3. Credit cards are not your friend, and the credit card industry is a trillion-dollar industry for a reason.

Chapter Twelve

It's A Whole New World

Maybe you have been working for six months, ten years, or even thirty years, however long you have been in the workforce it has changed from a decade ago. I remember when I first was laid off I immediately started to update my resume. I updated it because I needed to make sure it was perfect before I began to send it out to companies on every online job search website. I sent at least fifty resumes a day and filled out job applications to go along with those resumes. I sat in front of a computer screen eight hours a day until my eyes could no longer take the glare! Eventually I landed another job, but not before I sent out one thousand resumes and over four months had passed!

Gone are the days that you can send resume after resume through your computer to some unknown person and expect to get a job. The way the job market has been recently your resume might not even be seen by a human! If you are at a point in your life where you are unemployed looking for a new career or you are at a job you hate and want a new job then you have to recognize that it is a whole new world in career searching. You have to be ready to try new avenues that you have never thought about before!

You can still send a thousand resumes if that makes you feel comfortable, but you also need to try a few other tactics. You will have to be familiar with social media and also be comfortable tapping into your network! By hitting every one of these angles you will find it easier to land the career and pay that you want.

So many people look at social media as a way to keep up with family or tell the world what you ate for breakfast. That is a small part of social media and that part of social media will not help you get a new job or help you bring more money into your bank account. The first social media platform that you need to be familiar with is LinkedIn. LinkedIn is where your resume comes to life because you are able to do more than just put the bullet points of your career down. LinkedIn allows you to list any publications or articles you have written during the length of your career. Also you can list the strengths you have that may be beneficial to the hiring manager at your future job. LinkedIn gives you the opportunity to share your expertise in a certain area or areas.

For example you currently work in healthcare, but you want a higher paid position in the healthcare field. Within LinkedIn you would share healthcare articles, write about healthcare subjects, and comment on healthcare articles that other people post. When you take these steps you will begin to catch the attention of people in that field and those people may be looking to hire someone like you! LinkedIn is a professional website and you must stay professional at all times! Your profile picture should be taken by someone else and you should be dressed professionally. Women should wear a blouse with a suit jacket and men should wear a button down shirt, tie, and suit coat. This picture should be a headshot only and it should be uploaded to your profile before making the profile available for others to see. Make sure to connect with others in the industry you want to work for or can help you get to the position you want. If you need more help there are LinkedIn classes in most cities and many of those classes are free!

Twitter is another social media platform that can be used to find a new career. Whenever I mention Twitter to audiences I speak in front of a lot of the crowd frowns at the fact that Twitter can be useful. Twitter currently is a great place to find a new career, part time job, financial advice, and so much more! There are accounts on Twitter that only share open jobs for people to apply to if interested. These accounts posts jobs twenty four hours a day everyday!

Another way to use Twitter to your financial advantage are to follow people at the company you want to work for and participate in Twitter chats that your industry has on a weekly or monthly basis. If you want to be in education at any level there is a weekly chat you can join. Do you want to work in the media or government there are chats that only discuss those industries. You can participate in the chats or you can just read the tweets and learn! Chats are also a great place to find potential LinkedIn contacts. While reading through twitter chats search the names of the people within the chat on LinkedIn and if they are in a position to help you professionally then that is a person you would connect with on LinkedIn.

Social media is one way to get your resume in front of the right person. The other way is through your network! Have you ever heard the saying "it's not what you know, it's who you know?" Well, it is really about who knows you! I know Oprah Winfrey, but Oprah don't know me! What do you think would happen if I emailed Oprah for an interview? Nothing! That email would not even get to her! Your network determines your net worth so who actually knows you and can help you get to where you want be financially.

Start thinking about where you spend majority of your time each week. If you are employed and looking for a new job you are obviously not going to talk to people at your current place of employment, but there may be someone who no longer works there who could help you. Also reach out to people who you went to high school and college with that may already be working in the industry you are interested in. Church is also a great place to use your network and usually there are people from numerous industries in attendance every Sunday! The point is to talk to those who already are familiar with you and have no problem handing your resume to the hiring manager.

By attacking your career from different angles you are able to increase your chances of the right person seeing your resume and your talent. So many resumes don't get pass the initial screening online so you need to be able to reach the right person another way. It will be a lot easier for you to contact a hiring manager at Apple through

LinkedIn then it would be sending that manager a resume. I am not telling you to stop doing what you know, I am just giving you a few more options that will get you closer to your goal!

No More Bosses

Maybe your goal is not to have another boss, but to be your own boss. You have worked for someone else long enough and you are ready to start your own business and enter the land of entrepreneurship. As an entrepreneur myself I want to let you know that it will not be easy, but if you want it bad enough and prepare for it financially you can be your own boss! This book is set up to help you pay off all of your consumer debt (car loan, student loan, credit cards, payday loans, etc) so that you are in a better place financially in your personal life.

In order to be an entrepreneur you have to make sure your personal finances are in order so that your business can last. If your personal finances are terrible then eventually you will start to borrow money from the business and that is a sure fire way to find yourself with a boss again! When you are getting out of debt that is the time to start working your new business on the side to see if there is a market for the business. Are there people that are willing to pay you money on a regular basis?

You can not make a decision to leave a job that pays your bills for a business that makes you money like it is a hobby. You need to grow that business on the side to the point that if you were to quit your job and work your company full time then you will equal or surpass your current income! Remember that the energy company and water company does not care if your business has a bad month. They are still going to want their money! That is why it is so important to pay your debt off and have savings in the bank! If you want to truly be an entrepreneur your "ICYABF" should have a year's worth of expenses saved. This will make sure that you don't make bad business decisions because you are desperate for money.

Debt Sucks A-ha's

1. If you want a new career or higher pay you can no longer send out 1000 resumes and hope someone calls you.

2. Social media allows you the opportunity to get your resume in front of the right person quickly.

3. Use your network of people who know you to get your foot in the door.

4. Entrepreneurship is not easy and you must be prepared before you commit to your business full time.

5. Have a year's worth of expenses saved in your "ICYABF" before quitting your job!

Chapter Thirteen

The Time Is NOW!

Nothing I wrote in this book matters if you don't take action! None of this is rocket science. All it takes is you making it up in your mind to say enough is enough and then do the steps outlined in this book. Within this book I have given you step by step of how we paid the $50,000 of debt off in two and a half years. You may have more debt than we had or you may have less, but whatever the amount the steps and the process is the same. If you follow the steps and don't give up you will find yourself in a different place financially soon.

That first night at that dinner table was an extremely sad night. Jon and I were worried and the financial stress was weighing heavily on us. We were the parents of a one year old and that one year old was depending on us to grow up and to grow up fast. That night we made a decision to admit that we had failed financially, but we were not going to let that failure define our future. We decided that our tomorrow would not look like today and because of that decision our today looks a lot different.

We now have two children and only one of those children experienced the two and a half years of hard work it took to pay off the debt. Our other child never knew the struggle of being in debt and she never will! Today, sitting at the same dinner table has a different feeling. No longer are we eating in silence because Jon and I are worried about bills. No longer is one person at the table eating alone because the other is out making money with a part time job. No, today that dinner table is filled with smiles and laughter. It is filled with plans for our next vacation or the next charity we want to give to. Most importantly it is filled with peace.

Chapter Fourteen

How To:

1. Buy A Car Without A Credit Score

2. Buy A Home Without A Credit Score

3. Travel Without A Credit Card

4. Complete Your Dream Sheet

5. Complete Your Spending Plan

In the "Power Of NO!" chapter I talked a lot about staying away from credit cards. While you were reading that section were you thinking to yourself well how am I suppose to live? That is why I added the "How To" chapter so that I could show you how I live my life with a debit card only. Before I do that I want to tell you what your FICO score consists of so that you have a better idea of how your credit score is calculated. 35% of your FICO score is your payment history so how long you have been paying on debt. 30% of your FICO score is the amount you owe on your debt. 15% of your FICO score is the length of your credit or debt history or how long have you been playing the debt game. 10% is any new credit or debt you have and the last 10% is the different types of credit or debt you have. So what does your FICO score measure? It measures how great you are at giving other people your hard earned money. What doesn't it measure? It does not care about how much money you save. It doesn't care about you being free from debt and building wealth! If you are going to live the "Debt Sucks!" lifestyle then you have to rethink your relationship with credit cards.

Buy A Car Without A Credit Score

The car dealership does a great job at convincing us how much we need the newest car with the highest price tag. The commercials give us all the features of the car and makes us feel left out if we are not rushing to the dealership to take out a car loan. If you go to buy any car and have to take out a car loan then you will have to worry about your credit score. The only way to keep the car dealership from not running your credit is to not borrow money to buy a car. So how are you going to get the car?

You are going to pay cash for the car! So, obviously you are not buying the $30,000 car you seen on the commercial, but instead you are going to buy the used car that you saved your money to buy. There are plenty of used cars that are $4000 or less that will get you from point A to point B. When you purchase a used car not only do you save on car payments, but you also have lower car insurance and property taxes! You don't have to stay in a $4000 car forever, but you can save money each month and move up to an $8000 or $10,000 car in a few years. If you don't have to borrow money for the car you don't need a credit score.

Buy A Home Without A Credit Score

Not many people can put cash down for a house and pay for it in full. People who want to buy a home will more than likely have to borrow for the mortgage so they will need a credit score right? Believe it or not there are people with zero credit scores who are able to obtain a mortgage, but they have to take a few extra steps. Understand that you have to decide whether you are going to have a zero or a 700 credit score, but you can not be in the middle. You can not have a 475 credit score and think you are going to get a house. Thanks to the 2008 "Great Recession" those days are over!

If you want to get a mortgage without the worry of a credit score then there a few extra steps that you will need to take. You need to have four other credit lines with a twelve month payment history. That could be a cable bill, phone bill, car insurance, or utility bills. Also if you are renting currently you should have twelve to twenty four months of on time payments. Be able to show that you have been at your current place of employment for over a year and that your income can cover the mortgage. Last, but not least come with twenty percent of the down payment. For example if you want to buy a $100,000 home you should have at least $20,000 saved and that will make it more likely the mortgage will get approved.

Travel Without A Credit Card

I travel around the world with just a debit card. I rent cars, book flights, and book hotel rooms all with my debit card. When it comes to rental cars all of the top car rental companies will rent to debit card holders. What the rental car company will do is put a hold on your card for a certain amount of money and that depends on the company. It may be the entire cost of the rental or just a percentage.

The same type of hold will be put on your card when you stay at a hotel. If a hold is put on your card above the cost of the hotel or the rental car it will be released when you return the car or check out of the hotel. Using a debit card for a flight is very simple because it charges the full amount to your card when you book it. Traveling with a debit card should never be a problem if you have the money in your account!

DREAMS TO REALITY SHEET

Short Term: 6-12 Months

1.

_____

2.

_____

3.

_____

Intermediate: 3-5 Years

1.

_____

2.

_____

3.

_____

Long-term: 10-15 Years

1.

_____

2.

_____

3_____

Expenses

_____   _____

_____   _____

_____   _____

_____   _____

_____   _____

_____   _____

_____   _____

_____   _____

_____   _____

_____   _____

_____   _____

SPENDING PLAN EXAMPLE

Income:	Monthly	Annually
Wages		
Loan		
Alimony		
Child Support		
Dividends		
Total Income:		

Expenses:

Rent/ Mortgage

Car Payment

Groceries

Clothing

Eating Out

Gas

Cell Phone

Cable

Sewer/ Water

Electricity

Tithe/ Charity

Total Expenses:

Total Income

-Total Expenses

= Total Money Remaining

DEBT OWED

EX: Student Loan _____ $25,000 _____

_____   _____

_____   _____

_____   _____

_____   _____

_____   _____

_____   _____

_____   _____

_____   _____

_____   _____

_____   _____

Ja'Net Adams is an International Speaker and the author of the Debt Sucks book series. She has been called the "Money Attracter." Ja'Net has shown millions of people how to change their finances for the better so that they can live their dreams. She has spoken at corporations, college campuses, non-profits, and at professional organizations. Her advice has been featured in Huffington Post, USA Today, NPR Marketplace Money, Black Enterprise, JET Magazine, Biz Journal, USA Today College, CNBC, Fox Business, and so much more! Ja'Net's passion to help others win with money is the reason she is sought after all over the world!